Harpy Eagles

By Sandra Donovan

STECK-VAUGHN
ELEMENTARY · SECONDARY · ADULT · LIBRARY

A Harcourt Company

www.steck-vaughn.com

ANIMALS OF THE RAIN FOREST

Printed and bound in the United States of America
1 2 3 4 5 6 7 8 9 10 WZ 05 04 03 02

Photo Acknowledgments
Harpy Eagle Conservation Project/Kike Arnal, title page, 21, 22; Eduardo Alvarez, 8; Luiz Claudio Marigo, 16, 24; Root Resources/Kenneth Fink, 6, 11, 12, 14, 18, 28—29; Visuals Unlimited/John Cunningham, cover.

Editor: Bryon Cahill
Consultant: Sean Dolan

Content Consultant
Dr. Eduardo Alvarez
Harpy Eagle Conservation Project
Earthmatters.org

This book supports the National Science Standards.

Contents

MEXICO

BELIZE
HONDURAS
NICARAGUA

GUATEMALA
EL SALVADOR
Caribbean
Sea

COSTA RICA

PANAMA

ECUADOR

COLOMBIA

VENEZUELA

North
Atlantic
Ocean

GUYANA
SURINAME

FRENCH
GUIANA
(FRANCE)

PERU

AMAZON
RIVER

BRAZIL

BOLIVIA

South
Pacific
Ocean

PARAGUAY

CHILE

South
Atlantic
Ocean

ARGENTINA

URUGUAY

Range of the
Harpy Eagle

Surrounding
Land

Water

Borders

Rivers

N
W   E
S

A Quick Look at Harpy Eagles

What do harpy eagles look like?

Harpy eagles are among the largest eagles in the world. They have gray and white feathers and black wings. They have a double crest of gray feathers that stand up straight on top of their head. They have a hooked black beak and thick yellow legs.

Where do harpy eagles live?

Harpy eagles live in lowland rain forests found from southern Mexico to northern Argentina. They build nests in the tallest rain forest trees.

What do harpy eagles eat?

Harpy eagles eat only meat. They hunt and kill medium-sized animals, including monkeys, sloths, parrots, and toucans.

Harpy eagles have sharp claws that help them hold on to tree branches.

Harpy Eagles in the Rain Forest

Harpy eagles are among the most powerful eagles in the world. At almost half the height of a person, they are also the largest kind of eagle in South America.

Harpy eagles belong to a larger group of birds called raptors. Another name for a raptor is "bird of prey." Prey is an animal that is hunted as food. Birds of prey are birds that are very good at hunting. All raptors have hooked beaks and sharp claws.

The scientific name for harpy eagles is *Harpia harpyja* (har-PEE-yah har-PEE-jah). The name comes from the Greek word harpy. In ancient Greek myths, a harpy was a powerful monster with the head of a woman and the body of a bird.

This harpy eagle is sitting on a branch high in the rain forest canopy.

Where Do Harpy Eagles Live?

Harpy eagles live in the lowland rain forests of Central America and South America. Rain forests are places where many trees and plants grow close together and much rain falls. Harpy eagles may be found in rain forests from southern Mexico to northern Argentina.

Harpy eagles live among the treetops of the rain forest **canopy**. The canopy is the area of the rain forest with thick leaves and the most branches. The canopy is divided into lower, middle, and upper parts. The lower part is about 20 feet (6 m) above the ground. The upper part is about 100 to 150 feet (30 to 46 m) above the ground. Harpy eagles live in the upper part, about 130 feet (40 m) above the ground.

Harpy eagles have their own territories. A territory is land that an animal lives on and tries to keep for itself. Harpy eagles will fight other animals that try to enter their territories.

Scientists are not sure how large a harpy eagle's territory is. To answer this question, scientists from the Harpy Eagle Conservation Project put a small band around each eagle's leg. They also put special small radios on the eagles. The radios send out sounds that let the scientists keep track of the harpy eagle's movements. They learn how large a territory is by finding out how far away from its nest the eagle flies. They think a harpy eagle's territory may be 4 square miles (10 sq km) or larger. The eagles need a large territory to hunt in.

Aeries

Harpy eagles usually live in pairs of a male and a female. These pairs are called mates. Mates make an **aerie** to live in. Aeries are nests.

Mates look for a safe place in the rain forest to build an aerie. They usually build their aeries in the tallest tree they can find. These tall trees are called emergents because they are so tall that they emerge, or rise, above the tops of other trees. The trees must have thick branches to support the weight of the aerie.

To make an aerie, harpy eagles gather branches of all different sizes from the treetops. They often place these sticks in the fork of a tree. A fork is a place where a branch grows out of a tree trunk. They place the sticks so that there is depression, or hole, in the middle. Harpy eagles rest or lay eggs in the depression. They cover the bottom of the depression with leaves. When the leaves become old and dried, the harpy eagles will take out the old leaves and put in new ones.

Harpy eagle nests are very large. New nests are up to 3 feet (1 m) wide and about 7 feet

▲ This harpy eagle is building an aerie out of branches and twigs.

(2 m) thick. Each year, harpy eagles add more sticks to their nest. Over time, the nests can become so thick and heavy that they cave in. Then, the pair builds a new aerie.

Once a pair of harpy eagles has built an aerie, they will live in it for many years. Scientists have seen the same nest used for more than 20 years.

▲ This harpy eagle is stretching its wings. You can see its dark black feathers.

What Do Harpy Eagles Look Like?

Harpy eagles are about 2 to 3 feet (75 to 90 cm) tall. With their wings open, they can be up to 7 feet (2.1 m) wide. Female harpy eagles can be as much as one-third larger and heavier than male harpy eagles. Females weigh about 14 to 18 pounds (7 to 9 kg). Males weigh about 10 to 16 pounds (5 to 8 kg).

Gray and white feathers cover a harpy eagle's body. Their feathers on the head and neck are light gray. They have a double row of **crest** feathers on the head. A crest is a row of feathers that stick up straight from the top of a bird's head. Harpy eagles have white or light gray feathers on their front. They also have long gray tail feathers that help them steer and brake as they fly.

Dark black feathers cover the large rounded wings of harpy eagles. These wings are wide and short to help them fly quickly through the rain forest trees. Flying quickly helps the eagles sneak up and surprise their prey.

Harpy eagles have a large hooked black beak. They use the sharp beak to tear off pieces of food from prey. They also have powerful legs, which can be as thick as a person's wrist.

Harpy eagles have large yellow feet with long, sharp black claws. Claws on eagles are called **talons**. A harpy eagle's talons can be 5 inches (12.5 cm) long. This is as long as the claws of a grizzly bear. A harpy eagle's talons can carve deep grooves into the branches of trees that it often visits.

This harpy eagle is eating prey that it has caught.

What Harpy Eagles Eat

Harpy eagles are **carnivores**. This means they eat only meat from other animals. Harpy eagles are so strong that they can prey on animals that weigh as much as they do, up to 20 pounds (9 kg). Even if animals are holding onto branches, harpy eagles can grab them and carry them away.

Adult harpy eagles are top **predators**. A predator is an animal that hunts another animal for food. This means that the harpy eagle does not have natural enemies. Other animals are not strong enough to hunt and kill adult harpy eagles.

Harpy eagles eat mostly medium-sized and large animals, including monkeys and sloths. They also eat lizards, such as iguanas. Sometimes they may eat large birds, including parrots and toucans.

This harpy eagle has brought food back to its nest to eat.

Hunting and Eating

Many things make harpy eagles top predators, including their excellent eyesight. Scientists think that harpy eagles may be able to see seven times as far as people do. They can even see both forward and sideways. This helps them to spot prey from far away when they hunt.

Scientists also think harpy eagles use their sense of hearing to find food. Prey makes noise as it moves through the trees. Harpy eagles use these sounds to find the moving prey.

Harpy eagles hunt by sitting and waiting. They sit still on a high branch for hours at a time. When they spot prey, they swoop down to catch it. Harpy eagles can fly up to 50 miles (80 km) per hour. They often reach their prey before the animal even knows it is being chased.

Once the harpy eagle reaches its prey, it catches it with its large clawed feet. The talons are so sharp that animals cannot escape. Harpy eagles can stick their talons all the way through the body of a monkey or other large mammal. Then, they can carry their prey through the air and back to their nests to eat.

Harpy eagles use their strong, sharp beaks to tear meat from prey. Because they have no teeth to crush food, their body has a special part to help them digest. Digest means to break down food so the body can use it. This body part is a gizzard. Harpy eagles swallow small stones and other rough objects. These rough objects stay in the gizzard and help the harpy eagle digest food.

Scientists believe that harpy eagles mate for life.

A Harpy Eagle's Life Cycle

Scientists think harpy eagles mate for life. They will find a new mate only if the first mate dies. A male eagle begins to look for a female mate when he is about four years old. He tries to attract a female by calling. A harpy eagle's call sounds like a loud, long whistle.

Harpy eagles mate only once every three years. Soon after mating, the female lays one or two eggs. Usually only one of the eggs survives and hatches into a chick.

Eggs usually hatch in about 55 days. During this time, the mother usually sits on the eggs in the nest. Her body heat helps the chicks grow inside the eggs. This is called **incubating**. Sometimes the father sits on the eggs to give the mother a break. He also brings food to the mother.

Young

A chick has a special bump on its beak. It breaks out of its egg by tapping on the inside of the shell with the bump. After time, the tapping cracks the shell open. Sometimes it takes a chick more than one whole day to break out of its egg. When the chick first comes out of the egg, it is wet. It dries in about 2 to 3 hours. Newly hatched chicks are covered in down. Down is soft, fluffy feathers.

Once the chick has hatched, both the mother and father take care of it. A chick is usually very hungry, and its parents feed it something right away. The chick stays in the nest, and the parents fly back and forth with food. A chick can eat almost as much as its parents can.

To feed a chick, parents first eat the food themselves. The parents' bodies partly digest the food. Then, the parents bring the partly digested food back out of their bodies. They feed this soft food to the chick.

One scientist watched how a harpy eagle taught its chick to eat by itself. For many months after the chick was born, the parents would bring food back to the nest. They fed it to the chick. One day they brought food back, but did

▲ **This harpy eagle chick is covered with soft down.**

not feed it to the chick. The chick was very hungry that day. The next day, the parents fed only a little food to the chick. The chick was still very hungry. Finally, the chick started to eat a little of the food the parents left in the nest. A few weeks later, the chick was eating all by itself.

This eaglet is ready to fight anything that comes into its aerie.

Eaglets

A chick is in danger before it is able to fly. As it gets older, adult feathers grow in to replace its down. Until this happens, the chick will be unable to fly.

Parents leave the chick in the aerie to hunt for food. The chick may leave the aerie to explore the tree around it. Sometimes the branches are slippery. The chick may fall. If it does, the chick will die because it cannot fly.

After about six months, the chick has grown feathers and can fly. It is then called an eaglet. All eagles have special bones that help them fly. Eagle bones are hollow and filled with air. This makes them very light. The bones also have little braces running inside them. A brace is a strong, thick area of bone that supports the rest of the bone. This makes the bones strong even though they are filled with air.

Eaglets learn to fly by taking short leaps among the branches. They usually fly to branches that are on the same level as their nest. At first, eaglets usually stay close to their aeries. As they grow older, they may fly farther and to treetops that are lower than their aeries. After about one year, the parents teach the eaglets how to hunt.

Harpy eagles take care of their young longer than most eagles. After their first flight, young eagles stay in their parents' aerie for several years. Then, they leave to find a mate and build their own aerie. Harpy eagles can live to be 40 years old.

The harpy eagle is the national bird of Panama, a country in Central America.

The Future of Harpy Eagles

Today, harpy eagles are known as the kings of the rain forests. This is because they are so powerful that other animals cannot catch them to eat. Even so, harpy eagles are **endangered**. This means that they might die out.

Hunting is one thing that puts harpy eagles in danger. It is against the law in some places to hunt harpy eagles, but not in other places. People hunt harpy eagles for many reasons. Some hunters like to save harpy eagles' claws for trophies. A trophy is an object that is kept to show a success. Some people kill harpy eagles for food or to use their feathers to make things.

Harpy eagles have only one chick every three years. This means that there are not enough chicks to replace the harpy eagles that hunters kill.

▲ This scientist is studying a harpy eagle's aerie.

What Will Happen to Harpy Eagles?

Harpy eagles are also in danger because their natural **habitat** is disappearing. A habitat is a place where an animal or plant usually lives.

People are cutting down trees in the rain forest to start farms and to create roads and buildings. Harpy eagles cannot survive without their rain forest homes.

Harpy eagles can talk to each other. Scientists are not sure how much they can say, but they know that harpy eagles make certain sounds. They make short clicking sounds and long whistles. They repeat their whistles 8 to 12 times in a row. Scientists think these whistles can mean different things.

Scientists are working to save harpy eagles. By learning more about harpy eagles' territories, scientists hope to find out how they use the rain forest. They also want to know how much rain forest the eagles need to survive. Scientists can then try to stop people from building too close to harpy eagle nests. Other scientists are trying to hatch harpy eagle eggs. When the chick is an eaglet, the scientists release it back into the wild.

Some people are working to make hunting harpy eagles against the law in all Central and South American countries. Other people are working to stop people from destroying the rain forest. All of these things will help save the harpy eagle.

beak
see page 7

eyes
see page 16

wings
see page 12

tail feathers
see page 13

Glossary

aerie (AYE-ree)—a harpy eagle's nest

canopy (CAN-oh-pee)—the area of the rain forest with thick leaves and the most branches

carnivores (KAHR-nuh-vors)—animals that eat only meat

crest (CREHST)—a row of feathers that stand up straight on top of some birds' heads

endangered (en-DAYN-jurd)—an animal that might die out

habitat (HAB-i-tat)—the place where an animal or plant usually lives

incubating (IN-kew-bay-ting)—when a mother bird sits on her eggs so her body heat will help the chicks grow inside the eggs

predators (PRED-uh-turs)—animals that hunt other animals for food

talons (TAHL-unz)—long, sharp claws on an eagle's feet

Internet Sites

Animals of the Rain Forest
www.animalsoftherainforest.com/
   harpyeagle.htm

Harpy Eagle Conservation Program
www.earthmatters.org

Useful Address

Harpy Eagle Conservation Program
P.O. Box 15251
Gainesville, FL 32604

Books to Read

Kalz, Jill. *Eagles.* Mankato, MN: Smart Apple
   Media, 2002.

Merrick, Patrick. *Eagles.* Chanhassen, MN: Child's
   World, 2000.

Index